THE SECRET CLOCKS

TIME SENSES OF LIVING THINGS

SEYMOUR SIMON

ILLUSTRATED BY
JAN BRETT

DOVER PUBLICATIONS, INC.
MINEOLA, NEW YORK

To Joyce, Carmen, and the rest of the nice people at Equinox Travel

Copyright

Text copyright © 1979 by Seymour Simon
Illustrations copyright © 1979 by Viking Penguin
All rights reserved.

Bibliographical Note

The Secret Clocks: Time Senses of Living Things, first published by Dover Publications, Inc., in 2012, is an unabridged republication of the work originally published by The Viking Press, New York, in 1979.

Library of Congress Cataloging-in-Publication Data

Simon, Seymour.
     The secret clocks : time senses of living things / Seymour Simon ; Illustrated by Jan Brett.
         p. cm.
     Originally published: New York : Viking Press, 1979.
     ISBN-13: 978-0-486-48866-0
     ISBN-10: 0-486-48866-7
     1. Biological rhythms—Juvenile literature. I. Brett, Jan, 1949– ill. II. Title.
QH527.S46 2012
571.7'7—dc23

2012007602

Manufactured in the United States by Courier Corporation
48866701
www.doverpublications.com

Contents

THE SECRET CLOCKS

TIME SENSES OF LIVING THINGS

The Mysteries of the Fish and the Worm

It is a warm summer night. Thousands of people line the moonlit beaches of Southern California. They watch as the incoming tide pushes the waves high up on the sandy shore. The waters reach their highest point on the beach and then begin to recede.

Suddenly someone calls out, "Here come the grunion!"

As if by magic, the waves sweep wriggling masses of silvery fish onto the beach. Using their bare hands, men, women, and children scoop up one fish after another and toss them into pots, pans, bags, and other makeshift containers. Gulls compete with the people for the fish along the beach.

But there are plenty of grunion for all. In just a few minutes the pots and pans overflow with grunion. The gulls seem to be full, too. They eat more slowly, as if trying to find space for still another fish in their swollen stomachs.

As suddenly as the grunion run started, it is now ending. A few stragglers catch an outgoing wave and are gone. The sand is now empty of the slender fish. Some of the people on the beach set up fires to broil their catch right by the sea. Others head for home and backyard grills.

Everybody is talking about the grunion run and how it compared with the one two weeks ago and the one two weeks before that. Some wonder if there will be a second run tomorrow night or if the fish will disappear for another two weeks. Some of the old-timers talk about huge grunion runs of past years.

Slowly the beach empties as the campfires die down and people begin to leave. The beach is now deserted. The only sound is the regular boom of the breaking waves against the sand.

But the story of the mysterious grunion is not over. High up on the beach beneath the moist sand lie uncounted thousands of fertilized grunion eggs. They will be developed in about seven days. Even though the young grunion are ready to hatch, they will remain within the protective coverings of the eggs until two weeks have passed and the next half-monthly tides wet the sand around them.

Grunion are small, silvery fish that live along the Pacific Coast, from Monterey to southern Baja California, and in the Gulf of California. They spend most of their lives in the waters near the sandy beaches. But during their spawning season, from February to September, the grunion come onto the beaches as regularly as clockwork. Local papers actually publish the times when the grunion are expected on the beach.

The highest tides of the month occur during full moon and new moon, about every two weeks apart. Minutes before the night of the highest tide, the grunion swim in with the incoming waves.

The fish strand themselves as high up on the beach as possible. Wriggling about, the female digs into the wet sand, tail first. She lays her eggs about two inches below the surface. The male grunion curves his body around the female and spreads milt on the sand to fertilize the eggs.

The whole act of spawning takes only about thirty seconds. Then the grunion work their way back toward the water by flipping their bodies from side to side. The next wave carries the fish back down the beach. In two weeks the crashing waves of the next high tides will somehow signal the young, and they will hatch just in time to be carried out to sea.

Thousands of miles away from the grunion, the palolo worm lives in coral reefs around a few islands in the South Pacific. Palolo worms spawn only twice each year, in October and in November. The main spawning takes place during the last quarter of the moon in November. Scientists can predict the exact date each year. So, apparently, can the worms. Millions of them show up at the same time.

Adult palolo worms grow to be fifteen or sixteen inches long. They have two parts to their bodies. Just before they spawn, the hind part of the worm swells up with sex cells.

When the right day arrives, the hind parts of the worms soon shed their eggs and sperm, and fertilization takes place. Far below the surface the front parts of the palolo worms begin to grow new rear ends.

A year later the whole spawning act takes place again. At what is called "palolo time" by the islanders, the spawning worms are considered a food delight. They are scooped up by the bucketful, and great feasts are held. The spawning is so regular that the islanders date important events by it.

Many animals besides the grunion and the palolo seem to have some way of telling time within their bodies. Migrating animals start their journeys at the same time year after year. Most other animals follow a daily rhythm of activities.

Plants, too, have daily rhythms. Some flowering plants open only at night; other flowering plants open only during the day. Many plants show daily "sleep" movements; their leaves are erect during the day and droop at night. These sleep rhythms remain constant even if the plants are kept in constant darkness and at constant temperatures.

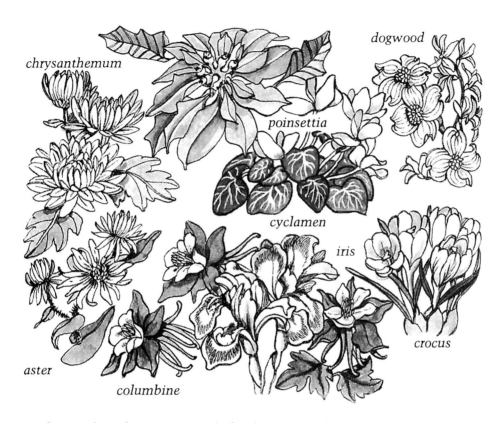

chrysanthemum

poinsettia

dogwood

cyclamen

iris

crocus

aster

columbine

Plants also show seasonal rhythms, much the same as animals. For example, poinsettias, cyclamen, and freesias blossom during the winter, while forsythia, crocuses, and dogwood blossom during the spring. Summer brings blossoms to iris, rhododendron, and columbine, while in the fall chrysanthemums, asters, and dahlias flower.

Humans also seem to have internal rhythms. Some people even try to chart their own.

Many of the daily, monthly, and yearly rhythms of living things have been known about for hundreds of years. But it was only when scientists such as Gustav Kramer of Germany began to study and experiment with animals and plants that these rhythms began to make sense.

Kramer was able to show that birds migrate in certain directions by using the position of the sun. He also showed that birds adjust for the sun's movement by using an internal rhythm that works much like a clock. Following Kramer's experiments, most scientists now use the term biological or internal clock when they refer to regularly timed rhythms in living things.

Each kind of living thing has its own ways of surviving and continuing its species. Each species relies upon some special features that help it to live and reproduce.

The giraffe's long neck and legs allow it to reach up to feed from the tops of trees where few other animals feed. The mouse escapes from many a close call with its enemies by being small and quick. The spines of a cactus protect it from animals that might feed upon it.

In much the same way the internal clocks of living things help them to survive. Birds migrate in just those seasons that help to insure them a plentiful supply of food. The internal clock of honeybees helps them to go in the right direction at the best time for nectar. Many plants open their leaves during the day and close them at night. In that way they receive extra sunlight and lose little water by evaporation.

Of course, the animal or plant does not *know* that its internal clock is helping it to survive. It simply continues to behave in the same way as others of its kind. By surviving, a living thing has a chance to reproduce and give rise to the next generation. Nature rewards survivors by allowing the continuation of the species.

What makes the clock of an animal or plant run so accurately? What sets these biological clocks and keeps them going? Do animals somehow learn how to keep time, or do they depend upon changes in their surroundings? What factors work to keep a plant on time?

In this book we'll look at some of the ways that scientists and nature observers have studied these questions. We'll examine some of their discoveries and some of the new questions the discoveries have raised. Later on you'll have a chance to try out your own experiments with biological clocks in animals and plants and even with the clock inside yourself.

Living Time

If you ever visit the lion house at the Bronx Zoo in New York, or any other zoo, in the early afternoon, you'll see something very strange. On a hot summer day most of the big cats are sleeping in their cages or moving around very slowly. But as it gets closer and closer to three o'clock, the animals start to pace restlessly back and forth.

There seems to be no reason for this activity unless you notice the sign on one of the cages. It says, "Feeding Time 3:00 P.M." Then the reason becomes clear. In some way the animals can tell when their feeding time is near and they become active. They do this long before they have seen their keeper approaching with their food.

Many people who have pet dogs tell a similar story. If they come home from work regularly at the same time, their dogs seem to be restlessly active and ready to greet them. But if one day they come home from work unexpectedly early, they may find their dogs resting or even asleep. The dogs' internal clocks are not set for their masters' coming home at that time. The dogs may even bark for a moment or two, as if a stranger were entering the house.

British naturalist Maurice Burton tells a story of the time sense shown by some stray cats in London. It seems that every Tuesday at noon a pet-food salesman would arrive with his wagon at a particular street corner in London. He would start to carve up meat for delivery to the cat owners in the nearby houses. While carving the meat, he would throw scraps and unwanted pieces to the ground for the stray cats which were around.

Soon cats would start arriving at the street corner every Tuesday just before noon for the handout. They would not come on any other day except Tuesday.

There are many other stories about what seem to be time senses in animals. Some of these observations date back hundreds of years. For example, the great Greek thinker Aristotle in the fourth century B.C. noticed that the reproductive organs of animals called sea urchins grew in size only during the period of the full moon.

Many sea animals seem to show changes that are closely connected with the phases of the moon. The half-monthly highest tides occur about fourteen days apart at full moon and at new moon. The palolo worm and the grunion are only two examples of many sea animals that breed during the time of the full moon.

Some animals, such as the robin, are early-morning risers and are active during daytime hours. Other animals, such as most bats, do the reverse. They get up at dusk and go to sleep at dawn. This helps each kind of animal find the food it eats — worms for the robin, flying insects for the bat.

Still other animals have clocks that seem to run on their own rhythms. For example, one kind of sea anemone opens and closes its many small tentacles over and over again in a kind of rhythmic slow-motion dance.

Many insects show different kinds of rhythms in their activities. In the tropics some kinds of insects bite only at particular hours. So if you are bitten at noon, you can assume it's probably one kind of insect; if you are bitten at three in the afternoon, it's probably another. This knowledge could help to prevent malaria or yellow fever if you knew when to protect yourself against the insects carrying the disease.

Even some microscopic-size living things seem to have time senses. There is a kind of alga, a tiny one-celled plant, that is phosphorescent — it gives off light. These algae are bright for twelve hours at night and much dimmer for twelve hours during the day.

At first it was thought that the algae were timing their phosphorescence to the light of the sun or to something else in their surroundings — temperature, for example. But the algae were brought into a laboratory and bred in aquariums in total darkness and under constant temperatures. Four hundred generations were raised under these conditions, so that they had never experienced daylight. Still they went on as before — twelve hours of bright light, followed by twelve hours of dim light. No one is sure of the survival value of this behavior.

Sometimes, however, it is easy to see how the secret clocks of animals and plants are of help in survival. For example, the males and females of birds that sit on eggs to hatch them will take over their duties on a fairly strict timetable. Female pigeons always sit on the eggs overnight until about eleven o'clock in the morning. Then the male takes over until about four or five o'clock in the afternoon.

Many other kinds of birds have remarkable time senses. One kind of bird called the tinamou lives in Panama, where it is called the three-hour bird. It breaks out into a song every three hours, day or night. It is said that Panamanians can set their watches by a particular tinamou's singing.

Birds will often gather at a specific time at a place where they are fed regularly. The birds do not wait for the appearance of the person who feeds them, but will gather before he comes. Starlings also come back to roost at the same time each evening.

Domestic animals seem to have time senses that fit in with human activities. Frank Lane, in his book *Animal Wonder World*, reports on several of these stories. One of Lane's friends had charge of a small herd of cows during a summer. He would feed them salt every Sunday morning. They seemed to like the salt, because every Sunday morning they would turn up at the right spot for the salt, but they would not come on any other morning.

In another story, a farmer, plowing a field with a team of ten mules, found that exactly at twelve o'clock, lunchtime, the mules would stop dead and begin to bray. It was useless to try to get them to move until they had been fed. At six o'clock in the evening the same kind of thing would happen. The mules would stop, begin to bray, and head in the direction of home. Talk about punching a time clock!

Farm dogs used for herding cattle or sheep are also very prompt. One such dog is reported to have gone off at seven in the morning and four-thirty in the afternoon to bring in the cows from the pasture to be milked. When daylight saving time came around, it took the dog a few days to adjust to a new schedule.

A chacma baboon kept in a Washington, D.C., zoo for twenty years followed its own work schedule. It would show itself in its cage until four o'clock in the afternoon and then enter its small room and close the door. It was finished for the day. Late visitors to the zoo would just have to come back the next day if they wanted to see the chacma.

Humans have all kinds of body rhythms. Many people wake up at the same time each morning just before an alarm clock is set to go off. Other people claim that they can adjust their internal clocks and wake up at any time in the morning they want to.

Even newborn infants show sleep and waking rhythms. These are generally short stretches of time at birth and gradually get longer until the twenty-four-hour stage is reached. Some infants show the same kind of activity — such as being fretful — at the same time each day.

While all these observations on biological time are very interesting, most of them are not very scientific — that is, they have not been tested or experimented with to see if any other explanations could account for the living thing's behavior. For example, could the dogs who seem to know the time simply be responding to something that the humans around them do at particular times? Let's take a look at what some scientists found out when they experimented with the clocks of living things.

Bee Time

Auguste Forel, a Swiss doctor at the turn of the century, often ate breakfast with his family in his garden on fine summer days. The breakfast table was set with fruit jams and jellies. Forel noticed that each morning honeybees would come at the same time to sample the sweets.

Forel thought the bees were attracted by the odor of the fruit preserves. But then he noticed something strange. Even when breakfasts were served in the house, the honeybees arrived in the garden at their usual time. Forel wondered if the bees could tell time in some way, but he never experimented to find out the answer to his question.

In 1912, just a few years after Forel's observations, a scientist began to experiment with bees. The scientist's name was Karl von Frisch, and he founded the Zoological Institution of the University of Munich. Karl von Frisch was to work all his life on the behavior of bees, and his discoveries would become world-famous.

In his early experiments Von Frisch put out dishes of sugar water and honey at the same hour each day. He quickly marked the first group of visiting bees with tiny dots of colored paint. Each day bees without the dots were caught and removed, so that only the group of bees with dots came back at the same time.

A timekeeper kept a record of each bee's arrival time. A large majority of the marked bees arrived at almost exactly the same time each day. When no food was set out, the bees still came at their usual time. Even after a week without food set out, the bees turned up promptly.

One of Von Frisch's students, Ingeborg Beling, went a step further in experimenting with the bees' clock. At first she simply trained groups of bees to come to a feeding station at specific times. She found that bees could be trained to come at any time during the day, or at several different times during the day. For example, bees could be trained to come at 7:00 a.m. or at 5:00 p.m., or at both 7:00 a.m. and 5:00 p.m.

Ingeborg Beling then tried something different. Instead of training bees to come at a particular time of the day, she tried to train them to come for food at a regular interval of nineteen hours. That meant that while the period between feedings remained the same (nineteen hours), the time of day would change. For example, one day the feeding might be at 7:00 p.m., the next day at 2:00 p.m., the next day at 9:00 a.m., and so on.

Ingeborg Beling found that the bees were absolutely unable to learn to tell any periods of time other than a twenty-four-hour period. Even when she tried to train the bees to come for food at the same time of day but at intervals of forty-eight hours, the bees were unable to learn to skip a day.

She concluded that the bees' sense of time was closely connected to a twenty-four-hour rhythm. Scientists call this a *circadian* rhythm. (The word "circadian" comes from Latin words which mean "about a day.") It seems that bees can easily tell the time of day, but cannot tell how much time passes in any period.

In nature, the time sense of the bees is important for its survival value. For example, many kinds of flowers have been shown to have daily rhythms in producing nectar. Bees have been found to visit the flowers at just the right times to gather the best nectar. The twenty-four-hour time sense of bees follows the same rhythm as the twenty-four-hour nectar production of flowers. But other periods of time, such as nineteen hours, have no importance for bees in nature. Thus it proved impossible to train bees to any units of time that were not based on a twenty-four-hour day.

Now that scientists knew that bees had a twenty-four-hour clock, the next question they tackled was what set the clock and made it work. It probably was not hunger, they thought, because bees eat food at any hour in their hives. Then to what changes in surroundings might a bee respond?

Ingeborg Beling thought about that question and came up with this list of possibilities. Bees might set their internal clocks by the changes in daylight and darkness or by the position of the sun in the sky. They might use changes in air temperatures, because days are usually warmer than nights. They might use changes in other weather factors, such as humidity or electrical charge.

To test these factors it would be necessary to eliminate changes in them. So a specially designed room was set up at the Zoological Institution at the University of Munich. Light, temperature, humidity, and other air properties were kept constant. After many experiments Ingeborg Beling found that the bees kept their clocks on time just as well in the laboratory as they did outdoors in natural surroundings.

But there were still other possibilities. For example, cosmic rays are a kind of radiation that bombards the earth and its atmosphere from outer space. This radiation could easily pass through the walls of any ordinary building. Perhaps bees were setting their clocks by the daily changes in the amount of cosmic rays reaching the earth.

To test this possibility, a hive of bees was brought down to a salt mine tunnel six hundred feet below the surface of the earth. Here cosmic rays could not penetrate. All the experiments were again repeated. The result? The bees still learned to come for food at any regular time as long as it was on a twenty-four-hour rhythm.

Only two explanations seemed possible. One was that the bees had a clock within themselves that kept going by itself. The other was that the bees' clock was set by some unknown force around them. But how could you test to find out which explanation was more likely?

Here was how Von Frisch and Beling reasoned. Suppose some unknown kind of radiation set a bee's time clock. Then the radiation must have a daily change in amount. The change could only come about in some way because of the earth's daily rotation. In that case the amount of unknown radiation would have to be linked to the position of the sun in the sky. So the radiation would be different from one place on the earth to another in a distant time zone. That was the factor that could be used in an experiment.

Von Frisch decided to train a group of bees on local time in Munich, Germany. Under controlled conditions the bees would be placed aboard a fast ship sailing to the United States. If the bees kept to local Munich time, then their clocks were within their bodies and not set by their surroundings. But if the bees shifted their feeding time as the ship entered other time zones, then their clocks were being set by some outside force.

Von Frisch quickly set up the experiment. A young student of his was to go aboard the ship to care for the bees and time their food gathering. Everything went as planned except for one thing. The

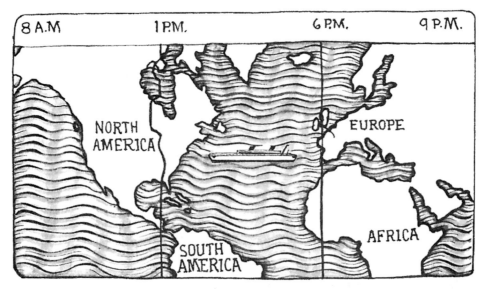

student observer became so seasick that she could not take a single note. Nobody knew what happened to the bees. Before Von Frisch could try the experiment again, World War II intervened.

Finally the war came to an end and the experiments were resumed. By 1955 fast flights across the Atlantic made the experiment much easier to try. Plane connections were best between Paris and New York, so it was decided to use those two cities. Identical sealed rooms were set up in both cities. The bees would be kept at all times in constant temperature, humidity, and light.

Max Renner, in Paris, and T. C. Schneirla, in New York, conducted the experiment under Von Frisch's direction. A group of forty bees were trained in the sealed room in Paris to feed between 8:15 and 10:15 p.m., Paris time. Then the bees were packed up and flown in a sealed box to New York. The journey was completed between feedings.

The hive was set up in the sealed room in New York, where it was five hours earlier daylight saving time. The scientists watched the hive carefully. If the bees came out to feed at 8:15 p.m. New York time, that would mean that their clock was controlled by some outside force connected with their position on the earth. But the bees did not wait. Twenty-four hours after their last feeding in Paris, at 3:15 New York time (it was 8:15 in Paris), the bees came out to feed.

So the experiment had come up with an answer. Bees do not rely on some outside force to set their clocks. Within themselves, bees have a clock that keeps on going regardless of outside forces.

But solving one mystery in science often leads to uncovering another mystery. We still do not know just how the bees' clock works.

Bird Clocks
and Compasses

Of all animals, birds are the greatest travelers. Nearly half of all the kinds of birds in the world migrate. The migrations of birds from one home area to another are usually seasonal, depending on changes in weather or in food supply.

V-shaped flights of migrating Canada geese are a common sight in spring and fall as the birds travel between their breeding grounds in the northern United States and Canada and their winter feeding areas in the south. Their journeys are spaced with familiar resting and feeding areas. Their high, lonely cries signal the coming of warm weather in the spring and of cold weather in the fall.

The champion migrating bird is the Arctic tern. Every fall these small relatives of the gull leave their nesting grounds within the Arctic Circle. For the Arctic terns which nest in Canada or Greenland, the first leg of their journey takes them across the Atlantic to the coast of Europe. During their transatlantic flight the terns neither feed nor rest.

A few weeks after their arrival in Europe, the terns are on the wing again. Their route takes them down the coast of Africa until they reach the cold, stormy waters around Antarctica. Here they spend the southern summer (it is now winter in the Arctic). To get to summer in the Antarctic the terns must fly at least eleven thousand miles. They make this incredible journey twice each year, from one pole to another and back again.

The tern, the Canada goose, and all the other migrating birds that travel great distances must have some way of pinpointing the place where they are going. Their internal compass must be able to rely on some kind of information from the outside world. But to just what kind of signals do migrating birds respond?

In 1949 Gustav Kramer, then at the Max Planck Institute of Marine Biology at Wilhelmshaven, West Germany, decided to try to find the answer to that question. Kramer had often watched migrating birds fly over the cold waters of the North Sea that bordered the Institute. The problem was that it was difficult to follow the direction of the birds' flight from a ground location. One scientist had learned to fly a small airplane and had followed some migratory birds. But that still did not reveal very many details about what outside signals the birds received.

Instead of following the birds in the field, Kramer decided to try a completely new way of experimentation. He knew that birds kept in cages become very restless during the migratory seasons. They seem to spend most of the time fluttering their wings against the cages in a particular direction. Kramer reasoned that this direction was the one they would take if they were free to fly. If that was so, then caged birds could be used in laboratory experiments to find out about migration.

Here is how Kramer set up his experiments. Kramer collected a number of young European starlings and raised them in large cages until they became tame. As fall approached and the days became shorter, Kramer observed his starlings carefully. (Kramer had to watch the starlings only during the daytime because starlings do not migrate at night.) From his laboratory the normal direction of starling migration would be to the southwest. Would the caged starlings flutter their wings near the southwest?

The answer soon became clear. All during the migratory season, the caged starlings fluttered their wings in the southwest corner of their cages. Now Kramer set about discovering why.

First Kramer moved the cages to a different place so that the starlings could not use familiar landmarks, such as a tree or a building. He also enclosed the bottom part of the cages so that only the sky was visible to the birds. No matter, the birds still fluttered in the southwest corner as before.

In the spring the starlings should be heading to the northwest. Kramer built a different kind of cage in order to be ready for the spring migratory season. The cage was a circular one made the same all around. A bird inside had no way of knowing one direction from another. There was a central perch so that a bird could fly in any direction from the center. The bottom of the cage was of clear plastic. An observer could lie beneath the cage and watch the direction of the bird's flight.

Kramer also wanted to change the direction and the amount of the

sunlight falling on the cage. To do that, Kramer built a six-sided house in which to hang the cages. Each of the six sides had a window, a shutter, and a mirror. The window and shutter could be opened or closed to light. The mirror could be used to reflect light into the cage at right angles to its normal direction. The cage could also be rotated in any direction.

All was in readiness for the spring migration season. Kramer observed his birds for at least an hour each day. Sure enough, the starlings spent most of their time near the northwest part of their cages. Kramer had proved that he could use his laboratory to study the direction of migratory flight.

Kramer now changed the conditions of his laboratory setup. He now used the mirrors to reflect the sunlight at right angles. To the birds in the cages it would seem that the sun was at a 90-degree angle to its real position. What would the birds do?

After many observations Kramer knew the answer. As soon as the position of the sun shifted 90 degrees, the direction of the birds' flight shifted 90 degrees. The birds corrected the direction by taking their bearings from the sun. If the sunlight came in from the correct position, the birds flew in the normal direction. But if the sunlight seemed to come from somewhere else, the birds changed direction to keep their bearings.

Kramer had shifted the sunlight 90 degrees in a clockwise direction. To make sure of what was happening, he now shifted the sunlight 90 degrees in a counterclockwise direction. The birds immediately shifted around 90 degrees counterclockwise.

Kramer now went a step further. He set up feeders with hidden food compartments all around the cage. After many days he was able to train a starling to look for food between 7:00 and 8:00 a.m. at the east side of the cage and nowhere else. When the bird was finally trained, Kramer moved the cage seven miles away from its original location. He put food in the east feeder, but at 5:45 in the afternoon rather than at 7:00 in the morning.

All during the training in the morning, the sun had been slightly to the right of the east feeder. Now, late in the afternoon, the sun was behind the west feeder. Would the bird go west in the direction of the sun? Or would it know which direction was east and go in the direction of the food? After a minute or two of fluttering around, the bird headed for the east feeder and its food reward. The bird was able to take into account the sun's movement during the day and go in the correct direction.

To make sure of what was happening, Kramer now decided to try still another experiment. He trained a starling in an outdoor cage to look for food in a west feeder at any time of the day. Next he placed a cover around the cage so that all sunlight was shut out. He then set up a strong light like an artificial sun so that it shone always from a position in the west.

The results were amazing. The starling continued to act as if it

were still seeing the real sun moving through the sky. Because the starling had been trained to look for food in the west at any time of the day, it now looked for food in the east at 6:00 a.m., in the north at noon, and in the west at 6:00 p.m.

In other words, the bird adjusted its direction just as if the sun were still moving. Somehow the starling was able to tell the time of day within itself regardless of its surroundings. Kramer proved that the only way that the bird could use the sun to tell direction was through the use of an internal biological clock.

Scientists were excited by Kramer's discoveries. In a few years they found even more evidence of internal clocks in birds. Dr. Franz Sauer of the University of Freiburg and his wife, Eleanore, decided to experiment with birds which migrate at night and are not able to use the sun.

They set up their cages in much the same way that Kramer had set up his. But they set up their experiments within a planetarium where they could project the stars on the walls. Despite the fact that some of the birds had been born and raised in cages, they tried to fly in the correct direction for migration by using the planetarium stars. When the Sauers shifted the position of the stars in the planetarium, the birds shifted also.

There is still much to be learned about how birds, without any previous experience in migration, know where to fly. But of one fact there is no doubt. Somehow, somewhere within many birds there is a biological clock. And this clock is so accurate that it can tell the passing of time almost as well as do the best human-made timepieces.

What Makes a
Secret Clock Tick?

You might not want to have cockroaches as guests in your house, but laboratories that work on animal clocks welcome them. Cockroaches are small enough to take up little room, but large enough to be easily dissected. They are tough and will eat practically anything. They live for many months and breed readily.

Cockroaches have been found to have a true time sense. They begin to run around just as darkness falls. For a few hours they are very active, and then they become quiet. The cockroaches remain quiet for the rest of the night and during the following day. As soon as it becomes dark, they begin their activities again.

If cockroaches are kept in a laboratory where the lights are left on for twelve hours and off for twelve hours, they become very regular in their circadian rhythms. Now suppose the laboratory lights are switched off six hours earlier one day and at the same time for the next few days. The cockroaches do not shift their clocks right away. They make up the time change gradually, by about an hour and a half each day. In just a few days the cockroaches are back on time with the lights. In this way it is easy to shift the cockroaches to be active at any times you want.

The same approach can be used with larger animals. In the Hall of Darkness at the Bronx Zoo, all the animals are usually active at night. But when bright lights are kept on during the night and only dim red lights are on during the day, the animals switch over and become active during daytime hours. This makes it easier for visitors to see the animals in action.

It seems clear that cockroaches depend upon periods of light and dark to set their clocks. But what do you think happens if the lights are left on for twenty-four hours a day and never shut off? For the first few days the cockroaches begin to run around at the time when the lights were formerly being shut off. But as day after day passes and the lights are left on continuously, the cockroaches begin to lose their sense of time. Sometimes they run at one time and sometimes at another. Since the cockroaches no longer have a circadian rhythm, they are said to be *arhythmic* (without rhythm).

The same kind of arhythmic cockroaches can be produced by keeping them in continual darkness from birth. But give such cockroaches even a brief flash of light, and they will immediately reset their internal clocks. Even if they are still kept in complete darkness after that, they will run on a normal twelve-hour schedule, at least for a number of days.

Temperature also affects the running of cockroaches' clocks. Cockroaches kept at temperatures cooler than 50 degrees

Some other animals that are active at night are the galago (top), the bongo (center), and the pangolin (bottom).

Fahrenheit (10 degrees Celsius) seem to lose their sense of time. Bees, too, have their clocks upset when they are kept at lower temperatures for periods of time.

Dr. Janet Harker, a scientist working at Cambridge University in England, has done many experiments on the internal clocks of cockroaches. Here are some of her findings:

Dr. Harker took an arhythmic cockroach and injected it with a drop of the body fluid from a normal cockroach. The arhythmic cockroach immediately began a twelve-hour rest and twelve-hour activity schedule. For a few days the arhythmic cockroach became normal.

There must be a substance produced by a normal cockroach that enabled it to set its clock. But just where was this substance made? Dr. Harker decided to try to find out. She experimented on many cockroaches by cutting out one or another body part. She knew that if she removed the correct body part the cockroach would become arhythmic.

Finally she tracked down the place in the cockroach's body that produced the timing substance. The source seemed to be in the second, smaller brain a cockroach has in the lower part of its body. The nerves in this smaller brain send out messages that control the movement of a cockroach's legs. When a cockroach starts to move in the dark, it is because a substance is produced in the brain that makes the brain send messages to the legs.

Dr. Harker found that certain brain parts from one cockroach could be transplanted. These brain parts from a normal cockroach could make an arhythmic cockroach begin to keep a normal time schedule.

Dr. Harker also tried to place brain parts of a normal cockroach into a cockroach whose clock was set twelve hours differently. What would happen when the cockroach received two completely different sets of timing directions from the brains? The answer was surprising. Dr. Harker found that the cockroach quickly developed cancer and died.

Not all scientists agree with the results that Dr. Harker found in some of her experiments. But it is clear that she has discovered much about how the internal clocks of cockroaches are made to tick.

Just when does the clock of an animal begin to work? Some experimenters used newly hatched chicks to find out. They placed the chicks in cages under constant conditions of light, temperature, and humidity. In just a few days the chicks started to show daily activity cycles of about twenty-five hours in length.

In fact, even before a chick hatches it shows signs of a circadian rhythm. Scientists found that the unhatched chick uses up much more oxygen (a needed gas) during daylight hours than at night. This is true despite the fact that the chick cannot see and only a slightly different amount of light would come through the shell anyway.

Some animal clocks may run slow or fast. One experimenter kept a flying squirrel under completely dark conditions. Normally this kind of squirrel becomes active about 6:00 p.m. In the constant darkness the squirrel became active about twenty minutes later each day. In other words, its internal clock was about twenty minutes fast. But in nature the squirrel's clock is normally adjusted every day by daylight and darkness. One kind of bat was even found to have a clock that ran twenty-two-and-one-half hours in the summer but twenty-five hours in the winter.

Perhaps the most surprising biological clocks are those found in an animal such as the cave crayfish. Cave crayfish live in caves that are in continual darkness and in which the temperature and humidity never vary by very much. This kind of crayfish has been living in caves for thousands and thousands of years. Yet the cave crayfish still shows a daily rhythm much like that of its surface relatives. The crayfish's internal clock keeps on running, although the crayfish's surroundings remain the same hour after hour, day after day, and year after year.

Sea Animals and Potatoes

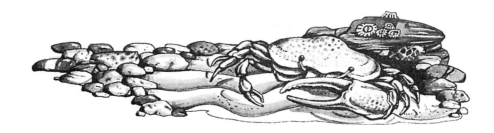

The fiddler crab is a funny animal to watch. The male fiddler crab has one claw that is much larger than the other. Its eyes are set on long, slender stalks that stand up way above its head. Fiddlers live in large colonies at the edge of the sea. Each fiddler lives in a burrow, which may be a foot deep.

The male fiddler sits at the mouth of the burrow, waving its big claw slowly in the air, for all the world like a musician playing a fiddle. The male is really trying to attract one of the nearby females. If a female fiddler responds to an irresistible male, she is led into the burrow. But if a person comes too near, the fiddlers all dash sideways and disappear into their burrows.

If you were to watch a group of fiddlers for just a few minutes, you would think that their colors are nothing special—light-brown, with purple and dark brown markings. But if you were to watch the fiddlers over the course of a day, you would see that their colors change. Between sunrise and noon a fiddler crab's body changes from a dark shade to a light one. In the afternoon the shade darkens again until sunset. The shade changes make it difficult for the crab's enemies to spot the crab on muddy beaches, which helps the crab survive.

Dr. Frank A. Brown, Professor of Biology at Northwestern University, was interested in the fiddler crabs' color changes. What would happen, he wondered, if the crabs were kept in a laboratory under conditions of continuous darkness and constant temperature? Surprisingly, the crabs kept in the laboratory continued to change colors at almost exactly the same times as before.

Professor Brown next decided to try keeping the crabs at different temperatures. He knew that most body changes are speeded up at higher temperatures and slowed down at lower temperatures. When the crabs were kept at temperatures with a difference of 35 degrees Fahrenheit, they still remained on their twenty-four-hour schedule of color changes. Even when kept for weeks or months in a darkened laboratory hidden from any sight of the sun, the crabs continued to change shade in time with sunrise, noon, and sunset.

In addition to their twenty-four-hour secret clock, fiddler crabs keep an entirely different kind of time schedule. This one is their feeding schedule, and it is set in time with the tides. At low tide the crabs are active. They search the beach for their food — little bits of animal or plant matter. At high tide the crabs return to their burrows and rest.

Would they stick to their tide schedule in a laboratory? Brown wondered. The answer was clear. When kept in a laboratory away from any natural ocean tides, the fiddler crabs became active at the times of low tides and quiet at the times of high tides. This was true week after week, even though *the times of the tides change each day*.

Tides are caused mainly by the moon's gravitational attraction on the earth. Animals in rhythm with the moon's movements are said to have a *circalunadian* rhythm. High or low tides occur twice every twenty-four hours and fifty minutes. In different places around the earth, tide times are different.

Brown next wondered what would happen if a tidal animal was taken to a distant shore. Would the animal continue to keep the tidal time of its home shore, or would it change over and respond to its new location?

The animal that Professor Brown decided to use for his new experiments was the oyster. Oysters were easier to observe than fiddler crabs because they had no feet and didn't run around. At high tide oysters open their shells widest, while at low tide they close up again.

Brown collected oysters from a Connecticut shore and had them shipped to a laboratory in Illinois, approximately a thousand miles away. They were kept in a darkened room in seawater. At first they continued to open their shells widest in time for high tide in Connecticut. But by the end of two weeks, the oysters had reset their circalunadian schedule. Now they opened their shells widest at the time that the moon would produce high tides if Illinois were on an ocean shore! In some unknown way the oysters had been able to reset their internal lunar clock.

Professor Brown's next series of experiments on internal clocks produced the most surprising results of all. For his experimental subject, Dr. Brown chose to use the common potato. Why the potato? For several reasons, said Brown. First, he wanted to use a common living thing that might show rhythms. If a lowly potato showed rhythms, he reasoned, then rhythms in more active living things certainly would seem likely. Second, he wanted to time a rhythm that many living things show, not like color change in crabs or shell opening in oysters.

Brown decided to measure the rate at which potatoes use oxygen in respiration. (Respiration is a life process common to almost all plants and animals.) He cut a short plug from a potato, keeping a single eye at the top. Each potato plug was placed in a small airtight container. Careful measurements were made of the amount of oxygen the potato took in each day.

When the observations were collected, the results were clear. Potatoes showed a definite twenty-four-hour rhythm in their use of oxygen. Even the lowly potato had a biological clock somewhere within itself.

But that was not all. Besides the circadian rhythm in the potato, Professor Brown found another, more unexpected result. It seemed that the potatoes changed the amount of oxygen they used according to changes in daily air pressure.

Weathermen use an instrument called a barometer to measure air pressure. Daily changes in air pressure are very useful in predicting changes in the weather. Professor Brown found that the potatoes were changing their oxygen intake two days in advance of a change in air pressure. In other words, *the potatoes could be used to predict barometer changes two days before they actually happened.*

In an article in the magazine *American Scientist* Professor Brown states that every living thing he studied in his laboratory, from carrots to seaweed and from crabs and oysters to rats, has shown changes in oxygen intake about two days in advance of changes in barometric pressure. A potato or a carrot that can accurately predict the weather two days in advance is better than many human weather forecasters!

Professor Brown did much of his research during summers in the Marine Biological Laboratory at Woods Hole, Massachusetts. One of the sea animals he worked with was a simple mud snail, the kind that, by the thousands, covers beaches at low tides.

Here is how Brown set up his experiments. He placed the snails in a small container, with an opening at one end, in a little water. Only one snail could fit through the opening at a time. As each snail left the opening, its angle of direction could be measured. Brown and his associates watched and measured the movements of more than thirty thousand mud snails over a long period of time.

When Brown looked over all these observations, he found a most peculiar pattern. The direction that the snails took depended upon the time of day. If the opening was to the south, the snails moved straight ahead at sunrise. But as the sun rose higher in the sky, the snails crawled more and more to the left side — in the direction of the sun. After noon the snails turned less and less to the left. Professor Brown also found that the snails followed the moon's motion in a similar fashion.

Professor Brown's results and ideas differ from those of many other scientists who are studying the biological clocks of living things. He believes that some of these clocks are set by both internal timers and some kind of external timer, such as the moon, the sun, or the earth's magnetic or gravitational field. Other living clocks, says Brown, are set simply by external timers.

Many other scientists in the field take a different view. They believe that some living things have internal clocks that go on ticking *regardless* of their surroundings.

Which of these two views is correct is not yet certain. Perhaps each of the views is correct for some living things. Much research is still going on. Perhaps one day the question will be answered. But without a doubt, the answer will raise many more questions for scientists to wonder about and to investigate.

The Times of Your Life

How would you like to run a race or take an important test at three o'clock in the morning? Do you think you would do better at these tasks at three o'clock in the afternoon? You're probably right if you chose the afternoon time. Most people do much better at that time.

At the Institute for Flight Medicine in Bad Godesberg, Germany, scientists tested people to see how they perform at different times of the day and night. The scientists measured body temperature, heart output, reaction time, and many other body variables. They gave their subjects many mental and physical tasks to perform.

Here are some of the things they found out: Mental performance on tests was best between 2:00 and 4:00 p.m. and good at any time between 1:00 and 7:00 p.m. Physical fitness and muscle coordination were also best at these times. Poorest performances occurred between 2:00 and 4:00 a.m.

These studies are important in deciding how to assign flight time to pilots and their crews. A pilot landing a jumbo jet should be alert both mentally and physically. The airlines try to arrange their schedules so that their crews are not faced with the most stress at the worst times.

You may have heard the term "jet lag." That's what happens to the passengers and crew on long east-west flights that go through many time-zone changes. A person with jet lag may develop headaches, lose his appetite, have stomach problems, and be tired yet not able to fall asleep. The same kinds of problems often occur with people who work night shifts or work at other odd times.

The reason for jet lag is that our body rhythms are thrown out of tune with our surroundings when we pass rapidly from one time zone to another. The clock in the airline terminal in London tells us that it is 10:00 a.m. while our body clocks tell us that it is only 5:00 a.m. Which do we believe?

Human body clocks seem to have many rhythms going on at the same time. Some we notice, such as our cycles of sleep and wakefulness. Others we may not notice, such as ninety-minute cycles of stomach contractions. Tests show that humans have more than one hundred different cycles going on all the time.

Most of these cycles seem to be related to four basic human body rhythms:

Ultradian is a ninety- to one-hundred-minute rhythm that the body goes through whether asleep or awake. (Ultradian comes from the Latin words that mean "beyond a day.") The first ultradian rhythms were discovered in sleeping people who showed periods of rapid eye movements about every ninety minutes. The sleepers also showed similar changes in brain wave patterns and muscle tension. Even when awake, humans go through ninety-minute peaks and valleys of feelings of hunger, periods of daydreaming and concentration, and many other activities.

Circadian is the more familiar twenty-four-hour rhythm. Not only do these include sleep and wakefulness, but also definite periods of high and low motivation and activity during both day and night. There are also daily rhythms in body temperature, blood pressure, and resistance to drugs and disease.

Circamensual are twenty-nine-day rhythms that are associated with the female menstrual period. (Circamensual comes from the Latin words meaning "about a month.") Definite physical and mental changes occur in females in a monthly rhythm. Research on possible monthly mood or body chemistry rhythms in males is now under way.

Circannual are yearly body rhythms. (Circannual comes from the Latin words meaning "about a year.") These may include seasonal changes in body resistance to disease, changes in mood and feeling, and even changes in rate of growth of men's beards.

The sleep-wakefulness rhythm has been studied by many people. In 1962 a young cave explorer named Michel Siffre spent two months alone in a cave in the French Alps. He had no clocks with him, only a tent, a small battery-powered light, food supplies, and a phone to the surface. The temperature in the cave was close to freezing all the time.

Each time Siffre awoke, ate, or decided to go to sleep, he would call his surface camp on the phone. The time of his calls and his words were recorded. In spite of the hardships, he held out day after day while spending his time writing a story about his adventures.

Throughout his underground stay, Siffre tried to keep track of the passage of time on the surface. When he was informed on September 14 that his two-month experiment was over, he was surprised. He thought that it was only August 20. He had lost twenty-five days.

But despite Siffre's confusion about the number of days, his body clock had kept on running. The times of his awakening and retiring calls to the surface were carefully checked. They showed that periods of activity and sleep on the average totaled twenty-four and one-half hours, just slightly longer than a day.

At the Max Planck Institute at Wilhelmshaven, West Germany, many studies have since been made of people in isolation. The subjects volunteer to spend at least three weeks in underground

apartments by themselves without any clocks or other time signals. Most of them show circadian rhythms of about twenty-five hours. It seems certain that the sleep-wakefulness clock keeps remarkably good time even without being set each morning by the rising sun or the alarm clock.

Still another daily rhythm that remains constant even in isolation is that of the body temperature. You may know that your body does not remain at the same temperature of 98.6 degrees Fahrenheit all the time. It varies about 1.5 degrees Fahrenheit during the day. Your lowest body temperatures are usually in the early morning hours, while your highest are in the late afternoon and early evening.

Of course people differ in their rhythms just as they differ in other ways. For example, some people think of themselves as early birds, while others think of themselves as night owls. An early bird wakes up with the sun and jumps out of bed all set to begin the day's activities. But comes the night, the early bird is tired and not able to stay up very late.

The night owl is just the opposite. He has difficulty in getting up in the morning. He much prefers to lie in bed until later in the day. But once the late afternoon and evening come, the night owl is in full swing. He can stay up to any hour without much difficulty.

Some people do not fit clearly into one or the other of these two types. At times they feel like early birds and at other times like night owls. Other people may get up a bit later but are able to stay up a bit longer too.

Scientists, studying these types, have found that each kind has a different temperature and blood pressure rhythm. The temperatures and blood pressures of the early birds rise and fall earlier in the day than those of the night owls.

The many body clocks of humans work in strange ways. Our clocks seem to be working even in events such as birth and death. Hospital records show that more babies are born between 1:00 and 7:00 a.m. than at any other time of the day. Even dying seems to be clocked. In a study of hundreds of thousands of deaths, the most common time of death was found to be 6:00 a.m., with a smaller peak at 4:00 p.m.

Yearly, or circannual, rhythms are more difficult to study than daily rhythms. After all, people may volunteer to be the subject to an experiment for a few days, but they are not likely to volunteer for a few years. Nevertheless, some studies of human yearly rhythms have been made, and the results are interesting.

For example, although popular wisdom tells us that a young man's fancy turns to thoughts of love in the spring, it's not true. According to studies made by several scientists, spring is a very difficult time of the year for most people. Suicide rates are highest in the spring, and people report that they are more depressed then. As far as love is concerned, a male's interest in the opposite sex reaches a peak in the autumn, and the same seems to be true of the female, according to Dr. Alain Reinberg of the Rothschild Foundation Hospital in Paris.

Robert Sothern, a scientist at the University of Minnesota's Chronobiology (*chrono* comes from a Greek word meaning "time") Institute says that men's beards grow more rapidly in the autumn and early winter than at other times of the year. He likens the beard growth to the thickening of fur coats in fur-bearing animals in preparation for winter.

Yearly human rhythms are difficult to identify. Over a three- or six-month period we are not likely to notice slight changes in one direction and then in another. Yet if we were to keep accurate records of changes in weight, appetite, sleep, mood, and work output, we might very well find clear circannual rhythms. It would not be surprising to discover that humans respond to seasonal changes just as plants, birds, insects, and other living things do.

Biorhythms
and Your Birthday

When Muhammad Ali lost his heavyweight boxing title to Leon Spinks, some people said they knew why: his biorhythms were at a bad point. The same people point to a "triple low" period on a particular day as having had something to do with causing Elvis Presley's death. They also think that many air crashes occurred because the pilot or copilot were at dangerous spots in their biorhythms.

Biorhythms supposedly give people enough information about their lives so that they will know whether they should stay in bed one day or go out and do something important another day. Some famous people, including well-known actors, sports figures, and business directors, believe in biorhythms. Almost all scientists, however, think that biorhythms are about as much use as fortune-telling with cards — a game to have fun with, but nothing more.

The theory of biorhythms states that simply by knowing your birthday you can make a chart that will predict the ups and downs of the rest of your life. According to the theory, you have three fixed rhythms in your life, each starting at the moment of birth. There is a physical cycle of twenty-three days, an emotional cycle of twenty-eight days, and an intellectual cycle of thirty-three days.

You are supposed to be able to do well in the up or plus part of each cycle, and badly in the down or minus part of each cycle. Half the days in each cycle are plus and half are minus. But the worst days are when the cycles switch from plus to minus or from minus to plus. These days come at the midpoint of each cycle. They are called critical, zero, or switch-point days. It's on these critical days that biorhythm believers say that you have to watch out.

If one critical day is bad news, imagine what might happen on a "double critical" day, when two cycles are at their midpoints and switching over. A "triple critical" day, when all three cycles switch over, is supposed to occur about once a year. On a triple critical day you're better off staying in bed, according to believers.

A critical day in your physical cycle is supposed to be the worst. For example, you might slip and break your leg. A critical day in your emotional cycle is not so bad. For example, you might have a fight with your friend. A critical day in your intellectual cycle is even less harmful than the other two. For example, you might do poorly on a test.

The theory of biorhythms grew out of the work of a German doctor named Wilhelm Fliess. Fliess was a good friend of Sigmund Freud, the famous founder of psychoanalysis, an important theory of behavior treatment. Fliess believed that the numbers twenty-three and twenty-eight were important in people's lives. Another doctor, Hermann Swoboda, was the first to make biorhythm charts.

Here's how you can figure out and chart your own biorhythms. All you need is a calendar, graph paper, and some math work.

Suppose you want to find out how your three cycles operate for the coming month. First you have to add up the total number of days in your life from the day of your birth to the first day of the month being charted. Now separately divide the total number of days by 23, 28, and 33. In each case, you will have a remainder of each cycle for the first day of each month.

Here's an example of how it would work. Suppose a person was born on August 9, 1968, and he wanted to find out his chart for the month of September 1979.

11 years at 365 days	=	4015 days
Extra days for leap years	=	2 days
Days from August 9 up to and including September 1	=	23 days
Total days	=	4040 days

Number of days from August 9, 1968, to September 1, 1979, is 4040. Now take the total days of 4040 and divide by 23, 28, and 33.

4040 divided by 23 = 175 cycles and *a remainder of 15 days*.
4040 divided by 28 = 144 cycles and *a remainder of 8 days*.
4040 divided by 33 = 122 cycles and *a remainder of 14 days*.

That means that the person would begin September 1979 with 15 days left on his physical cycle, 8 days left on his emotional cycle, and 14 days left on his intellectual cycle.

In the 23-day physical cycle, the first 11½ days are plus and the next 11½ days are minus. Since the person mentioned is 15 days into his physical cycle, he is in the minus stage. In 7 more days he will be at the changeover time and go into the plus state of his physical cycle.

In the 28-day emotional cycle the first 14 days are plus and the next 14 days are minus. Since the person mentioned is 8 days into his emotional cycle, he is in the plus stage. In 6 more days he will be at changeover time and go into the minus stage of his emotional cycle.

In the 33-day intellectual cycle, the first 16½ days are plus and the next 16½ days are minus. Since the person mentioned is 14 days into his intellectual cycle, he is in the plus stage. In 2 more days he will be at changeover time and go into the minus stage of his intellectual cycle.

If you don't have the patience to do all this adding up and calculating, there are a number of books with many charts that you can use for any days of the year. There are also pocket calculators available that do the job for you without your doing any figuring. There are even biorhythm services that, for a price, will provide you with your complete biorhythm charts.

If you were going to test to see whether biorhythm seemed to work for you, it would be best if you kept records of what happens with your physical, emotional, or intellectual states *before* you find out what your charts say. That way you won't be influenced by what is *supposed* to happen.

For example, suppose you rate yourself as strong to weak on a 10-point scale each day for a month. Also rate yourself each day on a 10-point scale from happy to sad. Finally, rate yourself each day on a 10-point scale from smart to dumb. At the end of the month find

your biorhythms and compare them with your ratings. Don't be surprised if they do or don't match up. It could happen by chance either way. A true scientific test would have to involve many different people during many months in order to determine whether or not the results were more than chance.

Some researchers say that their results show that biorhythms work. They report that twice as many accidents in a factory took place during critical times of people's biorhythms than during good times of biorhythms.

Other studies seem to point in just the opposite direction. They seem to find that just the average number of accidents happen during critical days of a person's biorhythms. In fact, Andrew Ahlgren, a University of Minnesota researcher who studies body rhythms, says, "Biorhythm theory is a silly numerological [number] scheme that contradicts everything we know about biological rhythms with their dozens of variables and differences from person to person."

If you think about biorhythms carefully, you'll understand why few scientists are even interested in studying the theory. Does it make sense that the exact date of your birth will schedule your behavior every day for the rest of your life? Body rhythms we certainly have. But biorhythms attached to three exact cycles and your birthdate seem to be as scientific as using the stars to predict your life on the earth — something no reasonable scientist would do.

Finding Out for Yourself

During the summer or during the warmer months of spring and fall, you can do a simple experiment to demonstrate the time sense of bees. Spread out some honey or syrup on a piece of blue paper. Place the paper outdoors each morning at the same time in the same spot. Bees can see blue, yellow, blue-green, and ultraviolet (a color you cannot see). The honey on the paper will attract the bees by its odor.

At first bees may not come to the paper. But as soon as a single bee discovers the honey, other bees are almost sure to appear. Continue to place the paper spread with honey in the same spot for several days after the bees start to come to feed. The bees will probably start showing up on schedule after only a day or two. In fact they may come a few minutes before you set out the honey.

After you are sure that the bees are showing up on schedule, place the same color sheet in the same spot but without any honey smeared on it. Start observing an hour earlier than the regular feeding time and continue for an hour later than the regular time. Record the number of bees that come in fifteen-minute blocks of time. Use a bar graph to show your results. (See the sample graph below.) Keep setting out the paper each day at the same time until the bees stop showing up.

You can realize that the bees must have a time sense if they show up a few minutes *before* you set out the paper with the honey. This is further demonstrated by the fact that they continue to show up at the right time even when the paper has no honey spread on it. The graph you make will show you how accurate the bees' time sense is. For example, in the graph below more than half the bees showed up within fifteen minutes of the correct time.

How do your results compare with those shown on the graph? For how many days did your bees continue to show up at the correct time? Try the same experiment at different seasons or at different times of the day to see if that makes any difference in the results you get.

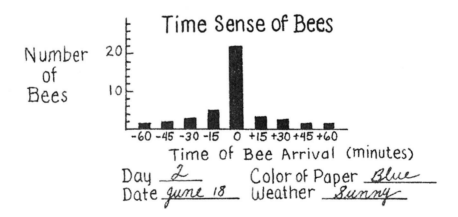

Try to observe any of the animal or plant timed activities mentioned in this book. For example, try to find a bird's nest in the spring where eggs are being hatched. (*Do not touch the nest or interfere with the birds in any way.*) Observe the actions of the brooding birds sitting on the eggs. (Note the times of the change-overs.) You will probably find that the male and female relieve each other at a regular time each day.

An hour before their regular feeding time, go to the section where the lions and other big cats are kept in a zoo. See if you can note a change in the behavior of the cats as their feeding time approaches. They may become restless and start moving about the cage even before their keeper is in sight.

Are there any other clues in their surroundings to which the cats may be responding? For example, the number of people watching the cats at feeding time is usually larger than at other times. Do you think the cats are responding to the size of the crowds? Would they respond the same way to a large crowd at another time of the day?

Try to observe fiddler crabs on a beach from early in the morning till late in the afternoon. The fiddlers' dark color should begin to get lighter until noontime. Note how the color changes help the fiddlers blend in with the muddy beach.

Also note the times when the fiddlers are running around and when they retire to their burrows. Where are the tides at these times? Remember that fiddlers are supposed to be most active at low tide and least active at high tide. Do your observations agree?

If you want to try an experiment at home with an animal's time clock, catch one small-size fiddler crab with a net. (Be careful of its large claw.) Place the crab in a bucket and cover it with several layers of damp seaweed. Collect several gallons of clean seawater in a plastic container, some clean beach sand in a bag, and a few flat rocks.

At home set up a large, shallow aquarium that has been thoroughly rinsed out. (Do not use soap or detergent for washing an aquarium.) Place beach sand at one end of the aquarium and keep it in place with some beach rocks. Pour enough of the seawater into the aquarium so that one side of the sand bottom is above the level of the water. Save the rest of the water by storing it in a dark place in a sealed plastic container.

Twice a week feed the crab a few small pieces of cut-up shrimp or fresh fish. Remove any uneaten food after an hour. If the water in the aquarium begins to smell, empty the aquarium, rinse it out, and set it up again with the reserve seawater.

Observe the color changes of the crab in the aquarium. Does it continue to change color at the same times of the day? Does it make any difference if you keep the aquarium in a sunny room or in a dark spot in the basement? If the crab keeps changing its color even when the aquarium is kept in a dark spot, what does that tell you?

Keep a record of the times that the crab is most active and least active. Check a tidal timetable for your area and compare it to the times of the crab's activities.

Do you know what time it is right now without looking? Even without clues some people can tell the time to within a few minutes at any part of the day. Of course, most people can tell you the time to within an hour or two by their daily activities — meals, school, TV watching, and so on.

Many people can wake up at the same time each morning even without an alarm clock. Even if they know that they must wake up earlier than usual one morning, they almost always find themselves getting up at the required time. Ask such people if they can explain how they do it.

See if you can guess how much time has passed for different periods. Have a friend check your guesses by timing you. Try to estimate when fifteen minutes, half an hour, or one hour have passed. Ask friends to try. Can you find someone who usually guesses very closely? Ask him how he does it.

Try to awaken yourself at a different time from the time you usually get up. For example, try to awaken one hour earlier. Just before you go to sleep, be sure to remind yourself of the time you want to wake up the next morning. Is your sleep more restless that night? Do you wake up and check the time several times during the night?

Ask your friends to try the same experiment. Compare their results with yours. Do any of them report that they do very well? Try changing the awakening times. Do the same people continue to do well?

One of your internal body clocks seems to regulate your body temperature. Use a mouth thermometer to read and record your temperature in the early morning when you awake, at lunchtime, at suppertime, and just before bedtime in the evening. At the times you take your temperature, try to keep constant conditions, such as activity and air temperature, around you.

Record your temperature for a few days at the same times each day. Do you see a daily pattern? Most people's temperatures are higher in the afternoons than in the mornings. Is that true of you? Ask your friends to try the same thing. How do their results compare? Are they similar to yours, or does each person seem to have his own temperature cycle?

Pulse rate, blood pressure, digestion, and many other body functions show daily rhythms. You might be interested in checking one of these, such as pulse rate. You can take your pulse rate in this way. Lay your left hand on a table, palm facing upward. Place the index and middle fingers of your right hand about one inch below the base of your left thumb. If you can't feel your pulse, move your fingers slightly and try again. The total number of beats per minute is called your pulse rate.

Record your pulse rate at different times during the day just as you did for your temperature. Again make sure that your activity and other conditions around you are kept constant. Does your pulse rate

Finding your pulse rate

seem to show a daily rhythm? Compare your results with your friends'.

Some kinds of plants flower in the spring, some in the summer, and some in the fall. The flowering time of plants seems to depend a great deal on the hours of sunlight compared to the hours of darkness. This kind of relationship of a plant to light is called photoperiodism (from "photo," which means light, and "period," which means time).

Some plants, such as the crocus and the chrysanthemum, flower in the spring or fall when the day length is long. These are called long-day plants.

Still other kinds of plants, such as the dandelion and the geranium, do not seem to depend upon the hours of sunlight. They flower at any time of the year, whenever they grow large enough. These are called day-neutral plants.

Try to observe the times of the year that plants flower in a nearby

park or garden. See if you can use a field guide to help identify the plants. Using your recorded observations, decide whether you think the plants are short-day, long-day, or day-neutral. Make sure that you understand the differences between each kind before you decide.

If you like, you can do an experiment with the time clocks of plants. You must start this experiment in the summer. You will need four large flower pots, some potting soil, cardboard boxes large enough to cover two of the flower pots, a roll of black tape, and two different kinds of seeds. One kind of seed should be either cosmos or dill or amaranthus — all from short-day plants. The other kind of seed should be either petunia or dwarf Shasta daisy or dwarf French marigold. These kinds of seeds are all from long-day plants. These seeds are commonly available in garden supply stores.

Fill the pots with soil. Follow the planting instructions on the seed packages. Plant about ten seeds from the first group in each of two of the pots and about ten seeds from the second group in each of the remaining two pots. Label each pot with the kind of seed you planted and the date.

Keep all the pots in a warm room that gets sun. Keep the soil in the pots moist but not soggy. You should get seedlings in about one week. When the seedlings are about two inches tall, pull out some of the larger and smaller ones so that you will have left about five average-size plants in each pot.

About four weeks after the plants sprout, place a cardboard box over one of the pots of the short-day group (such as cosmos) and over one of the pots of the long-day group (such as petunia). Use black

tape to cover all the seams so that no light gets through. Cover the pots each day about five o'clock in the evening and uncover them about eight o'clock in the morning. Continue to do this for about two weeks. Leave the other two pots uncovered at all times. Each day measure and record the height of the plants in each pot. Also record the day each plant flowers.

Compare the flowering time of the short-day plants in the covered pot with the flowering time of the short-day plants in the uncovered pot. Was the flowering time of the short-day plants affected by covering the pot? Did the uncovered short-day plants bloom? How do you know that the covering was the reason for the difference? Let the uncovered short-day plants grow for several more weeks until the fall. Do the uncovered plants bloom during the shorter hours of daylight in the fall?

The uncovered long-day plants from the petunia group will probably bloom during the summer, while the covered ones may not.

Can you explain why? If you remove the box from the long-day plants after two weeks, those plants will probably flower within a few days.

Most plants have to be healthy and large enough to flower no matter how much light they receive. So before you try these experiments, make sure that you care for your plants properly. That means using good planting soil, keeping the soil moist, and placing the plants in a sunny room.

In this book we have talked about only a few of the many human, animal, and plant rhythms known to science. It seems clear that there are internal clocks within most, if not all, living things. These hidden timepieces control and influence important life activities.

Without correct timing, many kinds of living things could not long survive.

We must recognize that human life is full of different rhythms. Like the crab whose color darkens with the rising sun, and the plant that flowers if given a little light, we also respond to changes in daylight, seasons, and weather. Just as with plants and animals, human internal clocks are in harmony with the rhythms of the earth.

SEYMOUR SIMON, whom the *New York Times* called "the dean of [children's science] writers," is the author of more than 250 highly acclaimed science books. He has introduced tens of millions of children to a staggering array of subjects in his books, which encourage young people to enjoy the world around them through learning and discovery, and by making science fun. Simon taught science and creative writing in elementary and secondary schools and was chair of the science department at a junior high school in the New York City public school system before leaving to become a full-time writer. "I haven't really given up teaching," he says, "and I suppose I never will, not as long as I keep writing and talking to kids around the country and the world."

For Further Reading and Research

BOOKS

Brown, F. A., Jr. *Biological Clocks,* Biological Science Curriculum Materials Pamphlet No. 2. Lexington, Mass.: D. C. Heath and Co., 1963.

Cloudsley-Thompson, J. L. *Rhythmic Activity in Animal Physiology and Behavior.* New York: Academic Press, Inc., 1961.

Gittelson, Bernard. *Biorhythm: A Personal Science.* New York: Warner Books, Inc., 1977.

Harker, J. E. *The Physiology of Diurnal Rhythms.* London: Cambridge University Press, 1964.

Luce, G. G. *Biological Rhythms in Human and Animal Physiology.* New York: Dover Publications, Inc., 1971.

Palmer, John D. *An Introduction to Biological Rhythms.* New York: Academic Press, Inc., 1976.

Reinberg, A., and Ghata, J. *Biological Rhythms.* New York: Walker Publishing Co., Inc., 1965.

Ward, R. R. *The Living Clocks.* New York: Alfred A. Knopf, Inc., 1971.

MAGAZINE ARTICLES

Aschoff, J. "Circadian Rhythms in Man." *Science,* 1965, Vol. 148, p. 1427.

Beck, S. D. "Insects and the Length of Day." *Scientific American,* February 1960.

Nelson, E. "New Facts on Biorhythms." *Science Digest*, May 1976.

Palmer, J. D. "How a Bird Tells the Time of Day." *Natural History*, March 1966.

—————— . "Human Rhythms." *BioScience*, February 1977.

Renner, M. "Time and Space in the Life of the Bee." *Natural History*, October 1966.

Time, February 27, 1978. "Those Biorhythms and Blues."

U.S. News & World Report, May 17, 1976. "In the Spring . . . "

Index